The Art of Self-Care

When Art Is Used For Healing

CICELY CARR

Printed in the United States of America
ISBN: 9798488262904
Imprint: Independently published

Kindred Creatives Art and Literary Press
2401 S Stemmons FWY #2130
Lewisville, TX
www.kindredcreativeszine.com

This book is dedicated to the creatives and the non-creatives and to those seeking peace as a lifestyle.

This book is dedicated to those that deal with stress, anxiety, depression, and other challenges that continuously run into walls and hard places.

This book is dedicated to soul searchers, survivors, and thrivers.

This book is dedicated to the sweet and soft souls.

This book is dedicated to the human being, the aliens, the mermaids, and the unicorns.

This book is dedicated to you, you are amazing!

Peace and Blessings,
CicelyRenee

table of contents

A MESSAGE

The Next 365 Days
Your Theme: Justice for Self
Focus: Inner Beauty
The Fruit: Enlightenment

I have a message for you. You have spent so much time focusing on friends, family, the country, and the world. You have cried many tears, felt many heartbreaks, and lost time. It is time sister to gather those tears, mend your heart and spend time with yourself! You need to fight for your life, your mind, body, heart, and soul. You are in control of yourself, and you haven't been playing fair. How can you pour from an empty cup? I implore you to spend the next year focusing on yourself. Not the outer you, but the inner you. What is inside will come out, and don't you want it to be genuine, healing, and oh so beautiful? The words that you speak will plant seeds in the hearts and minds. The behaviors and actions will water dry ground. Your being, your presence will fertilize giving fruit, big juicy sweet fruit in the lives of others. When you do this, focus on your inner beauty, you will tap into another realm of enlightenment that will elevate you and everyone and things you come into contact with. I can't wait sis!

-CicelyRenee

FORWARD

Mornings got so hard, I kept saying, "My bed is holding me hostage" which was a nice way of putting I don't want to do life today. The life stressed me out, it seemed to take me a long time to get it together so that I could drive to a job that sucked the life out of me. I came across a term, "functional depressions" I did what I needed to do to keep a roof over my head and to not drive over the cliff.

I spent my days at work, suffering from stomach aches and always feeling sick. I would disappear to gather myself. There was a time when I freaked out. I couldn't stop crying, I was overwhelmed, my heart racing and I had no idea why I was having my panic attack, I just knew I needed to leave.

My home was my sanctuary, I struggled with trying to be everything for everyone and not being everything for me.

Bipolar depression, that was the diagnosis. It made sense. My whole life I thought I was just a moody person, an empath. Always in a funk for no reason. They diagnosed me at 36 years old. This was after my journey of using art as self-care, creating became an addiction and when I couldn't do it due to work or other things I would get into that "funk".

This past year, 2020-2021, my "funks" began to go haywire which was the reason I decided to seek therapy. Some of the triggers were money, relationships, my job, loneliness and the biggest one, taking the risk to resign from my "stable" job while building a business feeling as if there just wasn't enough time. But now, I am a full-time creativepreneur with a bookstore. Releasing that job and pursuing art as self-care full-time through this bookstore and other avenues, I can say, I am in a much better position, thank God.

FORWARD CONTINUED

This book is a collection of thoughts, prompts, and techniques that address using art as self-care. This comes from 6 years of practicing as well as teaching classes that allowed people to explore thoughts, feelings and emotions through a variety of activities.

This was part of my daily routine and when it wasn't I would "lose" it and that was never fun.

I would encourage you to have a journal nearby or use the companion journal that is available.

I would encourage a minimum of 15 minutes a day to dedicate to using art or expressive arts as a way of self care.

If you can, carry a sketchbook with you everywhere you go along with some pretty pens or markers.

This is a lifestyle and would benefit everyone of all ages.

Please note that I am not a therapist and I am not diagnosing you, this is a daily habit that you could incorporate into your daily routines to make sure you are taking care of self in an expressive and visual way.

I hope this helps and encourages you to not only use it for self but share with others.

Sincerely
Peace

If you are pouring out to others all the time, make sure you take the time to fill up and pour into yourself. You have to take care of self first!

CICELY CARR

Part 1
Self Care

27 WAYS TO PRACTICE BETTER SELF-CARE

Self-Care tips and rituals saturate our news feed, our pinterest boards, our vision boards and more. It eats at our finances too! I realized myself and others fail at Self-Care, we are doing it all wrong.

Many times I see people talking about self-care and relate it to pampering, sure that's cool but self-care is so much deeper.

Self-care is making sure that you are mentally, emotionally, physically, and spiritually well before helping others. You may not be all well in every area, some need more tending to than others.

Many of us have gifts and talents that are not only for us but for others and the world. We all have a purpose that is so much bigger than ourselves but when we lack in self-care, you are unable to reach people and change lives due to mismanagement of self. When employees mismanage funds or jobs or people, they get fired, just like if we mismanage self, we could get fired too. The good thing, like a job, we get plenty of warnings, audits, check ins, observations and more. Our bodies are always talking and we just have to listen. Remember, our purpose is dynamic and not static.

Our bodies hold our minds, heart, soul and all that other gooey stuff in there. Many of us watch our loved ones, friends and family, struggle through life because of the things they let seep into them. Food, thoughts, people, activities, tv and more.

When it comes to Self-Care, it begins with a change of mindset and shifting your thinking. We are so hard on ourselves, we look at ourselves in such a negative light.

- Begin journaling for at least minutes a day
- Every time you say something negative about yourself, apologize, retract, replace with positive words
- Allow yourself to feel the emotions and go through the process of understanding it and living it out from start to finish
- Watch and listen to more empowering and uplifting shows, read books that will feed your mind and soul

When it comes to Self-Care, we tend to spend on things to make us feel beautiful like getting our nails done, hair and makeup too. We get massages or something else. That is cool, but...

- Go through your closet and get rid of things that don't make you feel beautiful
- Practice body positivity
  - Focus on areas you aren't the happiest with, stare in the mirror until you smile
  - Have a chat with yourself, ONLY good things
  - Take some photos of yourself and frame them
- Write love letters to yourself
- Post body-loving mantras around your house and read them anytime you come across them
- Workout at least 10 minutes a day- walking, dancing or anything that makes you smile

When it comes to Self-Care, we like to splurge on tasty treats, the newest shoes, or other things that we try to reward ourselves with. Like some people say, "Treat yo self"

- Everything in moderation, EVERYTHING- food, drinks, shopping, etc. well not drugs... drugs are bad but the other stuff, enjoy it on a regular
- Reward yourself with non-tangible things that will have a deeper meaning for you- give yourself a shoutout, plan a trip, eat lunch on the balcony or by candlelight
- Enjoy more rest or take a mental day off (My favorite)

When it comes to Self-Care, we think it is an event we sign up to once a month or year even.

- Be mindful all day everyday of your thoughts, feelings and behaviors
- Learn its triggers and keep track of it all the time
- Decompress for at least 15 minutes a day by journaling, drawing, sleeping, praying, meditating
- Find something you love to do or something you want to learn and practice it everyday

When it comes to Self-Care, sometimes we seek out validation from others.... or seeing them makes us do that comparison thing...

- Singles, maybe give the dating app a break (my current situation) thinking I would be happier if I had date or someone to kick it with
- Sometimes people don't need to know what you are going through because their advice sometimes can be more damaging
- Sometimes we may have to delete people on our friends list or profiles that we follow that alter our moods for the worse
- Forget what they think, give yourself advice
- Self-Care= Self-Love

Sometimes we think Self-Care tells us to get out the house...

- Maybe we can rearrange the house or just clean it- a messy house messes with my creativity
- Maybe bringing life into it by adding plants
- Create a space for your mental downtime

Time to start doing Self-Care the right way! It is more than an event, more than a "treat yo self", more than what others say it is... it is mental, emotional, physical, and spiritual but not 100% in each all at once. Show me someone who is and I will give you $5. Self-Care is a daily self-check in areas you want to focus on.

Challenge 1: Mindset

What you put in will definitely come out. What will you feed your brain? What outputs do you desire to come out of your mouth and actions? Why?

Books That I Want To Read   People That I Want to Research

Challenge 2: Self-Love

I dare you to spend the next 7 days, writing love letters to yourself!

Day 1

Day 2

Day 3

Challenge 2: Self-Love

I dare you to spend the next 7 days, writing love letters to yourself!

Day 4

Day 5

Day 6

Final Thoughts

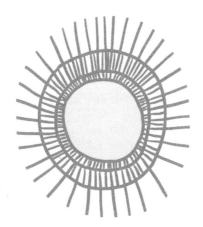

Challenge 3: Reward Yourself Sis

Plan your rewards! What are ways you want to celebrate your successes? What are the successes that you want to celebrate?

Challenge 4: Mindfulness

Mind over matter, if they mind... they don't matter... I think that was Jill Scott... or maybe Dr. Seuss either way... your mind needs to focus on what truly matters for you. What are some things that you want to focus on? What deserves more attention?

Challenge 5: Comparison

The comparison game is lame, there is only one winner, but there wasn't really a competition. Let's practice comparing ourselves to our past... notice growth, decline, or stagnant. What are your thoughts

Me Last Week

Me 5 Years Ago

Me 10 Years Ago

Me 15 Years Ago

Reflection

Challenge 6: Home

The home should be a sanctuary, solitude, your safe space. If it is, describe what is like to be in your sanctuary, what would you like to add or substract? If it is not your sanctuary, how can you make a space your sanctuary? Something you have access to 24/7?

Part 2
Journaling

10-7-5-3 REFLECTION JOURNAL
MODEL
BY
CICELY CARR

Have you ever struggled with journaling because you didn't know what to write? Have you googled prompts to help get your juices flowing? Have you given up journaling because you think you don't have the time? Well, I am here to help you with a model that you can use over and over that will help you create a routine that will then become a habit and ultimately becoming a lifestyle.

If you have been following me for a while, you know that I love reflecting and journaling. In fact, I love it so much I create journals so that you too can reflect and journal. I have the Pendrops and Doodles Gratitude Journal and my latest, Self A Self-Love Journal. You can find these on my Etsy Shop.

Journaling is a form of therapy. Imagine having a horrible day at work and because you want to keep your job, you keep some things left unsaid. Write it out, say what you want to say, feel free, and move on living your best life.

Journaling is a memory keeper. How many of you have diaries from your young days talking about all kinds of crazy things? Have you read them? Do you laugh?

Journaling shows change. Maybe you want to keep track of your moods and lifestyle changes. Maybe you want to see growth from you as a 25 year till 35, making sure you document everything
However you use your journal, remember it is a tool that can help you in so many ways!

So let me introduce you to the 10-7-5-3 Reflection Journal Model! Remember I am a professional educator, so I am always implementing strategies to help my students be their best selves in academics and life in general

When you think about journaling, it doesn't have to be an extensive amount of time. It can be short and to the point. However, you still may not know what to write.

10 The number of minutes you set your timer to! Don't stop writing until that timer finishes. Don't know what to write, well...

7 The number of things you thought about frequently that day or the night before. Could be people, events, your work, the things you have to do, things you want to do. What about those things?

5 The number of feelings or thoughts you have towards those things. Maybe a thing on your list is the doctor's appointment you have to set up and you are nervous for so many reasons. Maybe your list has a book that you want to read and you are excited about this author because they have so many raving reviews. So many thoughts and feelings, what to do with it next?

3 The number of questions you still have or profound insights that you stumbled across as you began your journaling

Part 2

7 Days Of
Journaling

SET YOUR TIMER FOR

MINUTES

7 Things On Your Mind

5 Feelings

3 Questions Or Profound Insights

Because You Might Have More To Say

7 Things On Your Mind

5 Feelings

3 Questions Or Profound Insights

Because You Might Have More To Say

_____

_____

_____

_____

_____

_____

_____

_____

_____

_____

_____

_____

_____

_____

_____

_____

_____

_____

_____

_____

_____

7 Things On Your Mind

5 Feelings

3 Questions Or Profound Insights

Because You Might Have More To Say

----

7 Things On Your Mind

5 Feelings

3 Questions Or Profound Insights

Because You Might Have More To Say

----

7 Things On Your Mind

5 Feelings

3 Questions Or Profound Insights

Because You Might Have More To Say

----

7 Things On Your Mind

5 Feelings

3 Questions Or Profound Insights

Because You Might Have More To Say

----

7 Things On Your Mind   **5 Feelings**

3 Questions Or Profound Insights

Because You Might Have More To Say

_____

_____

_____

_____

_____

_____

_____

_____

_____

_____

_____

_____

_____

_____

_____

_____

_____

_____

_____

_____

_____

Part 3
Using Art
for Self Care

ART AS HEALING

As a College and Career Coach for high school students I would help students find their passion when it came to careers. One of the amazing careers that would pop up was to be an Art Therapist. I thought this was a great career for people who loved to help people cope and also having a passion for art. As I talked students through this career to help them understand itbased on their strengths and interests, I two things crossed my mind, "I would love to do this as a career" and "There is so much healing in art."

What is Art Therapy

Art therapy is a mental health profession in which clients, facilitated by the art therapist, use art media, the creative process, and the resulting artwork to explore their feelings, reconcile emotional conflicts, foster self-awareness, manage behavior and addictions, develop social skills, improve reality orientation, reduce anxiety, and increase self-esteem. A goal in art therapy is to improve or restore a client's functioning and his or her sense of personal well-being. Art therapy practice requires knowledge of visual art (drawing, painting, sculpture, and other art forms) and the creative process, as well as of human development, psychological, and counseling theories and techniques. (American Art Therapy Association)

ART AS HEALING

Although, therapy is a word people tend to shy away from, just know that we involve ourselves in therapy on a daily basis and most of the time it is unintentional. You know the key things that help soothe you when you are stressed. Some of those things are positive and some of them can be negative. Positive things would be meditation, praying, tea, music, writing, etc. Some of the "negative" depending on your views could be drugs, alcohol, and other things. When it comes to more positive therapy options, you think about paying people to help diagnose you and guide you through issues. Well, I am here to tell you there are many ways to practice art therapy without having to hire a therapist. Although they may have a lot more resources and techniques, there are some of us that like to do it on our own terms.

DIY Art Therapy Tips:
- Create a space in your home- your sanctuary where you go to that specific place for peace, reflection, and connection. The entire home can scream chaos, children's toys all over the place, work that you brought home, dirty dishes piled up, whatever it may be, you need to a space that cuts all of that out so that you can focus.
- Carve out time- Whether 5-10 minutes a day or 2 days a week, dedicate time for your own personal art therapy time. Maybe right before bed to help relax you so that you can sleep better. Maybe it is right before work or having to cook breakfast.

ART AS HEALING

- Find things that you enjoy- My personal Art Therapy session is writing and DIY weekends. I look on Pinterest projects to do or try to recreate someone else's art. It could be having a playlist as you dance
- Be intentional- Anybody can color or play music but really digging into your thoughts and your feelings. You can focus on a series of statements or create according to your feelings and mood. Many of you create Vision Boards, which is a form of Art Therapy. Some ideas :
  - Paint a loss in your life.
  - Draw images of your good traits.
  - Design a visual autobiography.
- Keep track of all that you do- Ever look at your past journals and think, oh my gosh I have come a long way. Well, you want to be sure to keep track of your progress however that may look like.

Why You Should Embrace Art Therapy:
1. **Relieves trauma**- we experience trauma every day whether we are aware or not.
2. **Reduces stress**- we all know that stress is a major culprit to many diseases and we need to be well.
3. **Stimulates personal growth**- Cathy Malchiodi wrote in her book, The Art Therapy Sourcebook, " They may discover insights about themselves, increase their sense of well-being, enrich their daily lives through creative expression, or experience personal transformation."

THE VISUAL JOURNAL

The collector of amazing things

This journal can house many cool things such as movie tickets, letters, photos, cloth, paintings, and more. Each page can be its own theme or you could theme the whole book.

Sometimes we don't have all the words to express our feelings and emotions and visual journaling will help with that. From art to numbers to colors and more, learn ways to express yourself in a beautiful way. This short ebook will give you tips, prompts and more to help you fill our visual journal.

Visual Journaling allows us to SEE our thoughts. It allows us to tap into our feelings and what they look like. I like visual journaling because it allows us to create beautiful metaphors.

Visual journaling combines color and motion and connects it to our innermost parts.

Visual journaling helps us create a storybook of our lives to help us grow through, meditate and reflect.

So many of us feel as if we have to check boxes, abide by laws and regulations, follow a script or whatever, however life, there is no rule book, no step by step guide so do not feel as if you have to stick to any one thing. As we go through this ebook, you will be given ideas but you interpret it as you wish and create your own meaning.

COLORS

Color Meanings:
Red – danger, passion, excitement, energy
Orange – fresh, youthful, creative, adventurous
Yellow – optimistic, cheerful, playful, happy
Green – natural, vitality, prestige, wealth
Blue – communicative, trustworthy, calming, depressed
Purple – royalty, majesty, spiritual, mysterious
Brown – organic, wholesome, simple, honest
Pink – feminine, sentimental, romantic, exciting
Black – sophisticated, formal, luxurious, sorrowful
White – purity, simplicity, innocence, minimalism

Just know that your interpretation and experiences can define what certain colors mean to you. So there is no right or wrong way to express your feelings through the color choices you use.

SYMBOLS

Anything can be a symbol, your shoe, your purse, the cross and more. When you attach meaning to an object, idea, word or whatever, you create symbolism.

There are also so many very well known symbols that have become universal and can have both negative and positive connotations.

For example, guns, guns can mean protection for someone and danger to another. No matter the filter, neither is wrong or right, but it is their truth.

Symbols are in written and visual format.

Symbol Types

Animals- usually represent character and personality. Like an eagle, it represents leadership.

Colors- usually represent mood or feeling. For example, green represents growth, prosperity and more

Objects- usually represents memories or hopes. For example, a watch given to a son or the phone you keep looking at hoping for "the call"

Phrases- usually represents hopes and aspirations or negative or positive memories. "If you think you can you will!" "You will never amount to anything!"

Shapes- usually represent personality and character. The square mostly means a nerd. A circle is neverending.

There are so many other things that are symbols as well such as numerology or zodiac signs.

Thinking about these things can help you create meaning for your day.

Maybe you saw a series of numbers throughout the day. Sometimes I see the number 1234 about 5 times a week, so I will dig in and figure out what does this represents.

With my findings, I may reflect in my visual journal.

I may create a word art with the numbers and then write the significance and my reflection.

Being aware of certain things has made me so much more aware of my surroundings and the messages the universe or God sends to me!

So as you step into this visual journal lifestyle, make sure you pay much more attention to things that happen, how you feel, and what you see that you can create meaning to so that you can journal it later.

The next few pages will give us ideas on the whats and hows of filling your visual journal! This literally will be such a beautiful thing! So let's get started.

TYPES OF JOURNALS

Regular lined journal- Great for writing in but don't be scared to draw in it! Just because there are lines doesn't mean you have to abide by it!

Blank journals- great for drawing, adding your own photos, stickers, and more!

Painting journals and mixed media- feel free to add more than just a pen or pencil. Add paint, stickers, glue some quotes, add LAYERS and TEXTURES!

Build Your Journal- This is one that makes me excited, some call it junk journaling where they add things from all over to create more meaningful and creative ways to journal.

THEMES

Travel Journal- Are you doing a great deal of traveling? Document EVERYTHING! Take photos, add quotes, specify events and more.

Planning and Reflection- Whether it be wedding, school, major life events and more, this is a great way to track both small and huge events.

Art and Hobby Journal- Maybe you want to track growth and practice/reflect in one space when learning something new.

FAVORITE MATERIALS

When it comes to a visual journal, you want to incorporate even the craziest of things, for example grass from Italy.

You visual journal should never be flat, that is a rule and you may break it! However, to create a profound journal, you want to tap into the five senses as much as you can!

HEAR, SEE, SMELL, TASTE, and FEEL!

My favorite of these are FEEL! When adding to your journal, give meaning to touch!

As you travel, make sure you are collecting things that you could add to your journal. A bookmark, a ticket, a picture and more! This will definitely make your journal part of your life.

Art Supplies
1. Markers
2. Pens
3. Paint
4. Washi Tape
5. Magazines
6. Mail
7. Glue
8. Stapler
9. Paper
10. and so much more!

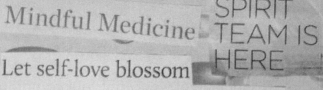
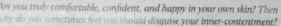
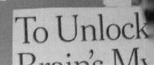
WHAT IT SHOULD INCLUDE

Intentions

I normally begin with an idea in mind focusing on a word, phrase, or feeling.

Images

These can be cut from a magazine, printed from the computer, or other

Lines

These add texture and give it depth.

Color

Splashes of color or vibrantly filled with color, it is up to you!

Background

Begin with plotting what the background would be, clouds, mountains, house, etc

Text

These are your thoughts or even just one word that you will add to the page.

Tips:

Layers

Textures

Memorabilia

Create a page and paste it in there

Live, Breath, Create, Repeat

Prompts to get the creative juices flowing! Your interpretation of how to respond to the prompt, is always right. If it says draw hope and you write a story about a bird, that is right! If it says to write about your feet and you draw a map, that is right! Prompts are here as guides and not rules to follow!

7 DAY VISUAL JOURNAL CHALLENGE

DAY 1: | Personal Creative Statement

DAY 2: | My Word Art
Find a word that defines your creative statement and make it pretty

DAY 3: | How You Feel about Creating

DAY 4: | Capture Something Beautiful

DAY 5: | Something That Makes You Angry

DAY 6: | Color Mood- Feelings and emotions carry colors... what is your color? Wat is connected to that color

DAY 7: | Capture something Weirdly Beautiful

MY TOP 10 VISUAL ART ACTIVITIES

1. Quotes I have heard and now I want to meditate on them through artistic ways
2. Color My Heart- choose colors that represent your mood and feelings
3. Power Word- Focus on a word that you want to embody
4. Objects that stood out to me throughout the day
5. Something somebody said to me that was profound.
6. Lists- I love lists whatever topic you want create a list!
7. Gratitude- write or draw things you were grateful for that happened today
8. Photos- capture and print a photo and write about it
9. Items from your day, maybe a ticket from a play, or a receipt from a first date.
10. Memories- Reflect about the past and write or draw your favorite memories.

Finish the sentence with "Creativity" in mind

I am

I will

I wish

I cannot stand

I regret

I plan

I should

believe

know

Lists- write at least 4 items in each category

Words to guide me:

I am my most creative when:

Creativity to me means:

The most beautiful things I have
seen are:

15 Challenges

1. Take photos of things or people that make you smile
2. Take a 30 minute walk in your neighborhood and BE PRESENT! Look at things around you, people and how they engage with others, the animals etc
3. Read or watch a documentary on someone you admire
4. Listen to an episode or few of How I Built This with Guy Raz TAKE NOTES
5. List 5 Influential People and why they are influential
6. List reasons why you chose those people and how it ignites creativity in you
7. Talk to 2 strangers... either online or people you cross paths with and interview them
8. Find an Anthem Song for you, write your favorite lyrics and what they mean for you
9. Create a Pinterest Board of all things INSPIRING- add pics, people, ideas, quotes
10. Brain Dump- Write for 15 minutes without stopping, editing, correcting etc... just write
11. Creative Playlist- Create a playlist of songs that you listen to and don't listen to, these songs should be uplifting and creative. Use this for remainder of challenge
12. Ask for advice, find someone you trust and ask about being creative, thinking outside the box etc
13. Find blogs or articles that helps inspire creativity, print them and post them
14. Find a hashtag for creativity, inspiration, good vibes etc and save your favorite posts
15. Sit in silence for 15 minute... let your mind wander try to remember things that your mind goes to

Part 4
Mind Over Matter

MIND OVER MATTER

Grounding Self
So many things, people, events, health, and more pull on us taking pieces of ourselves away. We hate our job and it's making us jaded, we can't get over this cough and it's making us miserable, we watch the news and we stop laughing as much. In this week's Mind Over Matter, we are GROUNDING SELF.

I have been having a sense where I feel so disconnected and not my normal self. I haven't been goofy, I feel withdrawn and I am just sad so often. This is because of stress due to work, finances and more. I realized I need to get back to self and that is where this topic came from. Grounding is a practice that can help you pull away from flashbacks, unwanted memories, and negative or challenging emotions. (Healthline)

Grounding Self is all about your **5 Senses, Hear, Taste, Feel, See, Smell and if you are all about that 6th sense, then spiritual.** Being intentional about this allows you to really be in the moment and be cognizant of your feelings, emotions, thoughts, and more.

Let's tap into our 5 senses that will help with Grounding Self.
Hear
- There are sounds all around us, take a moment to try to identify the sound, where it is coming from, and how it affects you holistically.
- Play non-lyrical music and try to hear each instrument on its own

Taste

- Grab your favorite drink and sip it slowly allowing it to glide on all your taste buds. Enjoy the flavors and feel how your body reacts.

Feel

- Lay in bed and roll around slowly, allowing you to feel the textures on your skin. Track your thoughts and feelings as you do this.
- Healthline wrote, put your hands in water and feel how it glides on your skin. They stated to do both cold and warm and connect with your emotions and mind!
- When in a stressful situation, find something near you and touch it, run your fingers over the textures, think about how it feels.

See

- Focus on a small part of a picture or an object, don't look at the whole thing, what questions start running through your mind? What do you see? Take in deep breaths and try to slow down your heart rate.

Smell

- I love going to bakery shops, take a trip to one, and sit there sniffing the air, breath in through your nose and out your mouth. What comes to mind? Memories? Happy thoughts?
- Take time to smell the roses, only if you like the smell and aren't allergic.
- Light incense or a candle and let the fragrance flood your space. Try to pinpoint the different essences of the fragrances.

There are so many other activities that you can do to help with Grounding Self. I encourage you to spend 5-10 minutes focusing on one or two activities. Grab your journal afterward and reflect on the experiences.

Create Happiness
On my laptop, I have taped, a little piece of paper that came from a fortune cookie. It reads, " Don't pursue happiness, create it!" It has been there for a few years, and what is funny is that I don't read it every day but somehow the words have pulled it into existence. I create happiness!

Many of us seek happiness through other people's actions. We sometimes seek it in unhealthy ways. We also live a life where most of the outcomes are out of our control and so with that mindset, we feel that happiness is so far from our grasp. But my dear lovely ones, happiness is closer than you can imagine.

One of the biggest things I struggle with on a daily is the fact that I put out so much effort and expect people to rise to the occasion. For example, as a teacher, I create amazing lesson plans, spending hours of my personal time writing these plans only to hardly get through it because of behaviors and lack of motivation. I feel defeated most days but then I realized, my happiness isn't dependent on how others take what I do for them. I do it because I love it despite the end results. Thus the epiphany:

Happiness is not the end goal but happiness is in the process.

EPIPHANY

Knowing that happiness isn't an end goal and it does not come from others, will help free you of unrealistic expectations, and will help jumpstart the creativity in happiness.

So this week's challenge is all about Creating Happiness and enjoying the process.

As you go through this challenge, make sure you are reflecting in a journal or some other medium. Capture feelings, thoughts, process,es and results. Focus mostly on the process, not the end result. What I am working on is not RUSHING, so join me on that.

Create Happiness Challenge
- Day 1: Back to the Basics- Focus on the simplest of things that make your heart happy. Is it sipping coffee in the morning? Is it getting cozy with your pillows on the sofa with nostalgic movies or soothing music in the background as you sway your hips back and forth. Basic can be beautiful and healing as well! Don't force it, embrace it.
- Day 2: Childlike- Remember no cares in the world, the world revolves around you! Use this day to put yourself on that pedestal, grab that candy bar, whine a bit, embrace the childlike mentally and be okay with it!
- Day 3: Bragging Rights-I don't know about you, but I struggle with tooting my own horn and you should be your biggest champion! Take the time to boost your own ego. Every time you pass a mirror, say something amazing about yourself! Check yourself out and just stare with the biggest smile!
-

- Day 4: Letting Go- Holding on to stuff both negative and positive will block new blessings. Letting go of notions, people, habits and more can help you be open to new and more profound opportunities. Take this time to focus on things you want to let go and enjoy and respect the process.
- Day 5: Live LAUGH Love- As a teacher, I feel forced to be strict and always make sure students are on their best behavior but many of them are so funny and sometimes I have to just let my guard down and laugh even if it is at an inappropriate time or just inappropriate period! Just laugh, be human. Take advantage of funny moments throughout your day. Reflect on what made you laugh!
- Day 6: Perfect Experience- I love looking into the future and painting my ideal situations! Take today and picture yourself at your happiest, who is around you? What are you doing? Where are you? What do you see? What do you look like? Write a letter, make a collage, etc to activate the plans and make sure the universe knows!
- Day 7: Eff the BS- Realizing that we don't control others and many things are out of our control will allow you to take a step back, breathe, and let things slide. I try hard to CONTROL my students, but in reality, they control themselves and I just have to deal with it. I can either stress myself over it or just let it go because at the end of the day, I go home to me, I have to take care of myself and they do them regardless. So I literally just have to shake my head and move on. Practice not being connected to others and what they do. Be cognizant of when you should just move on in situations.

Part 5
More Activities

LOSS THROUGH PHOTOGRAPH

Today I began my art session with a practice of circles and lines. As I did that, I connected with my thoughts. So many thoughts. It was silent, no music, just the sound of the heat blowing!

As I painted curves and lines of a familiar face, I was reacquainted with that person. The emotions and feelings began to replace the words, "I hate you" with phrases as to why such deep feelings.

I have been experiencing loss, having to let go, what a hard thing to do. Although I haven't completely let go, I can get a sense of a weight lifted being able to connect words with feelings.

As I practiced drawing this person from the photograph that I had, I looked at the background, I studied the curve of their lips and shoulders. I looked into their eyes and was transported to all the great memories that we had. The reason I hated you was because I miss what we had. Anger and rage was now vocalized and written and drawn on paper.

Once I was pleased with my drawing, more words came flooding out of my heart through my hand and wrote it next to the picture that I drew. I spent the next 10 minutes writing my feelings, the things I missed, and the final words, "I draw you so I never lose you."

Whether you lose someone or have to let go in any circumstance, that is hard! Many times we are inundated with the bubbles in our bodies filled with anger and pain but not able to vocalize how you truly feel.

This week, let's focus on losing someone whether you loved them or hated them and let's work on letting go through drawing them in a sense. Don't worry if you "cannot draw" this can be symbolic.

LOSS THROUGH PHOTOGRAPH

Letting Go with a Photograph

Part 1- The Set-Up

- Find your mediums- Paint, brushes, markers, charcoal, paper etc.
- Find your quiet place- Dining room table, desk, bedroom, closet, balcony, garage etc
- Begin with your intentions- What are you seeking in this session, be specific. "My intentions are to connect to why I am feeling this way." "My intentions are to connect with my emotions and let go of them." "My intentions are to connect with this person or thing so that I remember all the good memories."

Part 2- The Challenge

Challenge One- Portrait

- Study the photograph of the person or thing, the lines, the shades, the expression, the colors, the position, everything about it.
- Study how you feel when looking at it- does a smile grace your face? do your eyebrows shift down in anger? Do you begin tapping your foot or shaking your hand? What feelings are making your body to shift?
- Begin drawing what you see, the lines the shades, the colors just draw. Do not worry about if it looks like them or not. This is for your eyes only.
- As you draw or paint, what are you thinking about? What memories do you have? What dreams did you have? Goals and plans? Does this make you happy or sad? Angry or mad?

Title it- Don't write the name of them or it, but give it a title. "Popsicles in the Summer" "Ripples on the Lake"

- Reflect and Close- At this point, take a step back to look at the whole picture. Look at the small pieces, start from the bottom to the top. Look at bold lines, small lines, colors etc. See your feelings on paper. Think about that. You can ask yourself questions like, " Why did I use so little green when they are only wearing green?" Revisit your intentions, were they met or do you still need more? Validate your feelings, and then close the book.

Challenge Two- A Picture is Worth 1,000 Words

In this activity, you will look and study the photograph. If you did the first challenge, study that as well. You will then write, free-write. I would set a timer for at least 10 minutes and do not stop writing even if it is the same word over and over and over.

Suggestions on what to write:

- Words/phrases that come to mind
- "Reminds you of" metaphors and similes are great, think of a specific memory and go into detail of what it was like
- Write in detail a specific memory connected and how it made you feel.
- Write poetry, an essay, a song, a story…

Challenge Three- Collage

In this exercise, grab materials that hold memories, a ticket, a receipt, a piece of fabric, magazines, paper and more. Get a poster board, one of the small ones, glue, and scissors.

Different Ways To Approach This:

- What they represent- photos, shapes etc of what they represent for you. Is it hope or a prison? Is it debt or freedom?

What letting go looks like for you- are there clouds for freedom or a cave for feeling trapped?

- What you will miss about their presence
- After each challenge, make sure you take the time to reflect through thoughts, prayers, meditation, dance or whatever your medium might be.

Use this time to really own how you feel, use this as a sense of closure. Many times we never really get that closure in person so we have to have a symbolic type of closure and that is just as great.

Prompt:
The times I felt the most creative was when...
The type of people that inspire me to think on a deeper
level are, _____ and why?

Activities:
Earth
Take a walk in the woods, or around the lake, take time to
look at the flowers, the leaves, the trees, the dirt... Look
for messages.. listen

Wind
Focus on your breathing... breathe in the fresh air, let it fill
your lungs as you connect with the wind around you. Listen
to the wind... the music... feel the wind.. is it warm

Fire
Light candles or a bonfire... watch the flames, the shapes,
the smoke... listen to the flickering of the flames. Feel the
warmth... smell the aroma

Water
Slowly drink room temperature water and feel it as it
coats your mouth. Feel it as it glides down your throat.
See if you can feel the water that you are made of... your
muscles, the tears, your hair. Tell the water to hydrate dry
areas.

Part 6

Mantras

"I float in a bubble, it protects my peace of mind. Gentle and delicate, that's my peace. I will protect it."

CICELY CARR

Respond to the mantra

"The light in me shines bright, giving sight to dark roads. Those that come into my presence will feel the warmth of love and peace. They will be enlightened."

CICELY CARR

Respond to the mantra

"Bold looks amazing on me, confidence dangles on my wrists. Power on my feet with every step I take. I am fearless, my faith empowers me to walk in my purpose."

CICELY CARR

Respond to the mantra

_____

_____

_____

_____

_____

_____

_____

_____

_____

_____

_____

_____

_____

_____

_____

_____

_____

_____

_____

_____

"My soul is love. My heart has peace. My mind is still. I am light and love."

CICELY CARR

Respond to the mantra

_____

_____

_____

_____

_____

_____

_____

_____

_____

_____

_____

_____

_____

_____

_____

_____

_____

_____

_____

_____

_____

"I am planted firmly on the ground. No wind will knock me over. I stand tall for what I believe in. My foundation is strong."

CICELY CARR

Respond to the mantra

"I am my best friend, my biggest champion, my biggest cheerleader and I love seeing me happy. I make sure that happiness is an internal action and not dependent on others and events."

CICELY CARR

Respond to the mantra

"I have one body, one vessel, there are many cracks, but I am still whole. I put in fresh water, plant seeds that will birth greatness."

CICELY CARR

Respond to the mantra

"My mind, a powerful muscle yields inventions, creativity, it solves problems, it creates empires. My mind, a powerful muscle."

CICELY CARR

Respond to the mantra

"I turned the glass ceiling into bubbles, bubbles I float in, high into the sky. There are no limits stopping me. I have moved out of my own way. I elevate daily, always competing with yesterself, I am better, I do better. There are no limits."

CICELY CARR

Respond to the mantra

"I like a feather floating in the wind, falling slowly with beauty, suspense, and grace. I land softly on the shoulders of love, peace, and joy, the ride is nice, smooth, and so soft. I embrace softness."

CICELY CARR

Respond to the mantra

_____
_____
_____
_____
_____
_____
_____
_____
_____
_____
_____
_____
_____
_____
_____
_____
_____
_____
_____
_____
_____
_____
_____

"My strength comes from my passion, my love, my morals and values. I am resilient and call on my strength when I need that extra push to keep moving and surviving, better yet, thriving."

CICELY CARR

Respond to the mantra

"I have no control over others, just my everyday steps, my choices, my thoughts, my words... I choose to design a life that I love, that makes sense to me and that works for me. I am the master of my fate, the captain of my sea."

CICELY CARR

Respond to the mantra

"I have no control over others, just my everyday steps, my choices, my thoughts, my words... I choose to design a life that I love, that makes sense to me and that works for me. I am the master of my fate, the captain of my sea."

CICELY CARR

Respond to the mantra

_____

_____

_____

_____

_____

_____

_____

_____

_____

_____

_____

_____

_____

_____

_____

_____

_____

_____

_____

_____

_____

_____

Part 7
Closing

CLOSING

I remember one day while I was teaching, it was a rough day. The students were off the chain. There was drama between the administrators and teachers. Money was funny. I was hungry. I was frustrated. I NEEDED AN OUTLET. All I could think of was, "I can't wait to go home and create" That was my outlet. I created and there were no rules nor expectations. It provided peace, security, and many times something physically beautiful. Creating was my therapy, it was healing. I needed this to make sure that when I showed up for others, I was mentally, emotionally, and spiritually well.

As I close out this book, I hope that you have experienced and enjoyed peace. I hope that you explored thoughts and feelings through creating that you have not explored before. I hope that you continue this creative journey as a lifestyle.

Share this with others!

Peace and Blessings,
CicelyRenee

Made in the USA
Las Vegas, NV
21 October 2023

79459184R00056